TEEN MENTAL HEALTH™

anger and
anger management

Charlie Quill

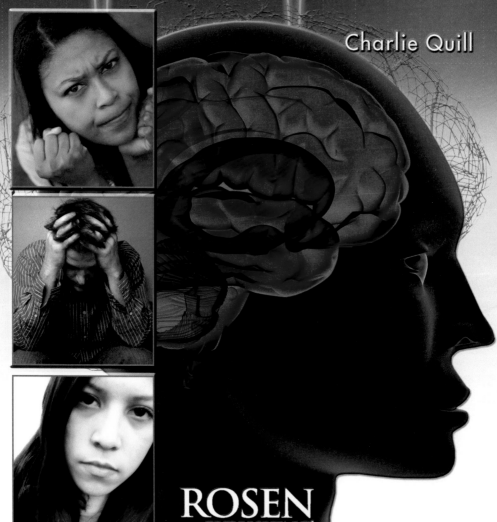

ROSEN
PUBLISHING®
New York

Published in 2009 by The Rosen Publishing Group, Inc.
29 East 21st Street, New York, NY 10010

Copyright © 2009 by The Rosen Publishing Group, Inc.

First Edition

Library of Congress Cataloging-in-Publication Data

Quill, Charlie.
Anger and anger management / Charlie Quill.—1st ed.
   p. cm.—(Teen mental health)
Includes bibliographical references and index.
ISBN-13: 978-1-4042-1800-0 (library binding)
1. Anger in adolescence. 2. Adolescent psychology. I. Title.
BF724.3.A55Q45 2009
155.5'1247—dc22

2008002953

Manufactured in the United States of America

contents

chapter one

The Basics of Anger

Anger is one of the most common emotions, yet it is probably the least understood. Everyone gets angry at one time or another. People get angry for many different reasons, some of us much more easily or more often than others. Being able to control your anger and knowing how to keep it from getting you into trouble are both very important skills. Understanding the underlying factors and emotions that trigger anger is also very important.

Sources of Anger

We are surrounded by images of anger in our daily lives. We see anger on the nightly news, on the front page of newspapers, in the movies, and maybe even in our own home. Most of the time anger is a negative force, but sometimes it can be used in positive ways. For example, in 1981 a terrible tragedy occurred for the family of John Walsh, host of the television show *America's Most Wanted*. Walsh's six-year-old son, Adam, was kidnapped and murdered. As you can imagine, this caused the Walsh family extreme pain and anger. What made things even worse was that there was no system set up in the United States to locate missing children. There was no one other than the local police to help the Walshes find their little boy.

Walsh and his wife decided to do something about the situation. Because of the Walshes and their anger, there are now laws in the United States that protect missing and abused children. There is also an organization for missing children.

John Walsh, host of *America's Most Wanted*, addresses television critics on a press tour in Pasadena, California, in 2006.

When Walsh was asked to host *America's Most Wanted*, he knew that this program could help catch dangerous people and keep them from harming others. Because of the Walshes, many missing children have been located and returned to their families, and many suspected criminals have been caught to face their charges.

Unfortunately, people lose control of their anger more often than they use it constructively. When this occurs, the people they love the most are usually the ones who suffer. Sometimes, people take out anger on their families simply because they are there. Your parents or other family members may get angry with you for things you do. And you may get angry with them, too.

Sometimes, anger in teens escalates into violence. In the most notorious case of school shootings, Eric Harris and Dylan Klebold went into their high school in suburban Colorado wielding guns. That morning in 1999, they killed thirteen people before they turned their guns onto themselves. Before the shootings, Harris had started a Web log in which he posted information on making explosives and aired threats against his teachers and classmates. He was clearly an angry person, and without having any effective mechanisms to deal with his anger, he and his friend decided to take it out on others and themselves. The Columbine High School tragedy is an extreme example of anger that spins out of control.

Anger and Stress

Have you ever found yourself with too many things to do and not enough time to do them? Homework, chores, social commitments? The following are fairly typical signs of stress:

- Feeling irritable or crabby
- Feeling tired and restless
- Acting jumpy, excitable, or "wired"
- Having a nervous, upset stomach
- Feeling paranoid, anxious, and extremely fearful
- Having strong feelings about small problems
- Getting confused or being unable to concentrate
- Doubting your abilities

Stress is unavoidable. However, learning new ways to deal with stress helps to limit angry outbursts.

There is absolutely no way to keep yourself out of stressful situations. They just happen. But you can certainly learn how to deal effectively with stress. It is also extremely important that you eat right, get enough sleep, and exercise regularly. All of these healthy strategies can improve your ability to handle stress constructively.

There are many things you can do to stay calm and gain control of yourself when you are angry. Try to think positively. Think of an upcoming stressful situation as an opportunity to learn and challenge yourself. When you need help because you feel scared and angry, you should find an adult to whom you can talk. Remember to take time out from a task that is stressing you. Do something relaxing, and take some deep breaths. Go back to your task only when you are ready to deal with it again.

A counselor or therapist can help you to relieve stress, often by simply letting you talk about what is bothering you.

Turning Anger Inward

Angry feelings that are turned inward can be very damaging. For example, Kurt Cobain, the lead singer of the 1990s grunge rock band Nirvana, had a lot of anger. Cobain had many serious problems, including a heroin addiction. His anger helped him with his music by providing a theme for some of the lyrics in his songs. And because of his songwriting and guitar playing, he was able to work through some of his inner problems and use his anger positively. Unfortunately, songwriting was not enough to get rid of his anger. In 1994, he killed himself. Cobain left behind a wife and a young daughter. In the end, they, too, were victims of his anger. Cobain's suicide shows how sometimes suppressed anger can lead to self-destructive behavior.

Oftentimes, depression in adolescence can look like irritability, and it is often misdiagnosed as anger, according to the *Diagnostic and Statistical Manual of Mental Disorders*. In these cases, treating depression is necessary, and anger management won't be effective. If you think that you may have depression, you should see a therapist for diagnosis and treatment options.

Great Expectations

Some people who are actually very talented at many things tend to be too hard on themselves. If they do poorly on a test at school, they call themselves stupid. If they miss a basket in physical education class, they call themselves clumsy. They might say things to themselves

9

like, "I'm never going to get anywhere in life because I can't do anything right." The more these people tell themselves such things, the more they believe them and the less they try to do anything at all.

Sound familiar? These people suffer from low self-esteem. Low self-esteem is one of the biggest causes of anger among young people today. Many psychologists believe that extremely low self-esteem can even drive a teen to commit crimes of violence. Teens with a healthy self-esteem will not experience as much anger.

Parents and other adults can help to build young people's self-esteem by being supportive, not critical. Love and firm support will always motivate somebody more than harsh criticism and complaints.

Frustration, disappointment, and sadness are confusing feelings that all teens must face at some point.

Frustration

Have you ever heard the expression, "Life is what happens to you when you're making other plans"? There are going to be times in your life when you can't get what you want. Accepting this idea is a big part of growing up. Not getting what you want can be very frustrating, and you may vent your frustration on the people who care about you.

As you know, the teenage years can be difficult. Many changes are taking place. Your emotions are changing with the rest of your body. You are exploring new feelings. These changes are not bad; they are necessary for your development. But changes mean that there are new things to learn about yourself. If you are feeling angry, look closely at your other feelings as well. Ask yourself:

- Am I under stress of any kind?
- Do I feel threatened somehow?
- Is someone (or something) important to me at risk?
- Do I feel frustrated or discouraged?
- Am I setting realistic goals for myself?
- Am I thinking about my failure in the wrong way?

Answer these questions first. You may be able to understand why you are feeling angry. Finding out why you're angry can be the most important step. It can keep you in control. It can help you feel like you have the power to solve your problems.

chapter two

Reacting to Anger

There is no escaping the fact that we live in a world that can be hostile and violent. More young people in America today die from gun violence than from anything else. In recent years, arrests for homicide (murder) among juveniles have increased dramatically. More than five thousand hate crimes (crimes motivated by prejudice against a group of people) are committed in the United States every year.

These are some negative results of anger. When people can't control their anger, or they bottle it up inside for a long time, it can become destructive. Destructive anger can emotionally or physically hurt other people and is not considered socially acceptable.

The Brink of Rage

Most people have a certain boiling point at which they lose their temper, no matter how well-adjusted they might be under normal circumstances. What distinguishes those who can "deal" from those who can't is how they handle themselves when they are on the brink of losing control. Martial artists often speak of being "mindful" at times when you feel emotion has taken over and common sense and good judgment are nowhere to be seen. What they are saying is that despite the powerful feelings that may take hold of you during a time of great stress, you need to remember not to let these feelings cause you to act out in inappropriate ways. The best way to handle this type of extreme anger—or rage, really—is becoming aware of escalating anger before you let it loose. If you feel that you are at the brink of uncontrollable anger, you need to first cool off and then address what caused you to get so upset in the first place later. People rarely think clearly when they're in a rage. And if you can't think clearly, you can't possibly make good decisions.

That being said, this kind of anger can be hard to handle, so if you do need to hit something, try a punching bag in the gym—not the nearest locker or your best friend or the family pet. Remember, you are responding to something or someone you don't like, and the only thing you can control in these situations is you. Maybe the best

The Hulk represents the rage, aggression, and violent impulses that are inside every human being, waiting to be released.

thing is to go off by yourself when your feelings become too strong to control. Find a private place to "explode." Scream, kick, or jump up and down—whatever it takes to calm down—without hurting yourself or anyone else.

Violence

Violence is one way to express very strong feelings. It is the use of physical force to injure or abuse someone or something. Some people become violent when they are angry. If a person is very angry, has a mental illness, or is high on drugs or alcohol, he or she might become violent without even realizing it. For some people, violence may be a normal response to anger. They may not have learned how to control anger. Perhaps the anger has been kept inside and not expressed for a long time. It is important to learn to deal with your anger in ways that aren't violent. More often than not, violent people cause pain to themselves and to people and things they care about.

Sometimes, a person becomes violent when he or she blames another person for something that has happened. The angry person can't cope with the emotions and feels that he or she has to punish someone else. The person chosen to be punished may not have anything to do with the problem at all. This is usually the case when a parent abuses his or her child. The parent is angry about something else and may be unable to resolve the problem that is causing the anger, so he or she takes it out violently on the child.

A person can suddenly respond to anger violently—without warning. Or, anger can build up slowly over a period and then suddenly explode. A person can lose control. There is no way to predict the actions of a person with this much anger.

Violence in Schools

Since the mid-1990s, there has been a slew of notorious school shootings. Although there are many theories on what caused these young people to hurt or kill themselves and

Cho Seung-Hui perpetrated the Virginia Tech massacre in April 2007. The killer's writings, self-portraits, and video recordings revealed a lifetime of bottled-up anger.

others, the common theme is that they were all unhappy and angry. When anger isn't addressed and when young adults don't know what to do with the strong feelings of anger that they carry, they may turn to extreme measures as an outlet.

Keep Your Cool

When someone "loses it," it means they are "letting it all out." This letting go of anger can be emotional or physical, or both. This kind of anger can also be hurtful. The purpose of this kind of anger is to let off steam. Sometimes, in letting go of anger, the person may also lose control. Here are some examples:

- Acting hostile toward others when you don't get your way
- Slamming doors or punching walls
- Hanging up on a friend who tries to give you advice
- Throwing clothes around your sister's room when you discover she tore your favorite blouse
- Yelling and swearing when you hit your thumb with a hammer
- Driving recklessly while trying to catch the car that cut you off

Passive-Aggressive Behavior

Have you ever heard the expression "If looks could kill"? A nasty look or violent gesture sends a pretty plain message.

17

Anger is frequently expressed with harsh words, threats, or actual physical violence, but often it is felt by others in more subtle but equally destructive ways.

Passive-aggressive behavior is a method of dealing with stress or frustration in which the angry person attacks other people in subtle, indirect, passive ways. Resentment, stubbornness, procrastination, sullenness, or intentional failure to do requested tasks are good examples of passive-aggressive behaviors. For example, people who are passive-aggressive might deny they're upset with you, but their demeanor toward you makes their true feelings plain. Some of the common passive-aggressive ways in which anger is expressed include gossiping about others, being overly critical, holding a grudge, the aforementioned dirty look, and, last but not least, the "silent treatment."

chapter three

Anger and Self-Esteem

Do you know someone who gets angry about everything? The smallest things become huge issues, and then everything spins out of control. Or, maybe he or she always thinks the worst of a situation, no matter what the circumstances. There can be many reasons for this person's bad attitude, but one of them is probably low self-esteem. People who have low self-esteem don't feel very good about themselves. They often feel as if they are the victims of everyone else's wrongdoings. People who have high self-esteem genuinely like themselves and are much better at taking and accepting responsibility for their problems. If you don't like yourself, it will be hard to like others. When you become angry, you may react violently.

The Role of Puberty

Many young people start to lose confidence in themselves during their teenage years. There is great pressure at school. You want to please your parents, but you also want to fit in with your friends. It's hard to make the right choices all the time. You begin to doubt yourself. You listen to that little voice inside you that says you are a failure. No matter what other people say, you don't believe that you've got much worth or talent. Your self-esteem gets lower.

Depression

Depression very often follows low self-esteem. People who are depressed have many physical symptoms. They don't have much energy. They stop taking an interest in the things they used to enjoy. They may not care how they look, whom they see, or where they go. Depression affects the body and the mind. It can cause people to believe that they are ill, or it can really make them ill.

When people stop believing they have value, they may become self-destructive; they turn their anger inward. They may think they are not worth being treated well or may even start believing that they should be treated badly. They may find boyfriends or girlfriends who abuse them. They stay with them because they think they don't deserve any better. Or, they may abuse their own bodies by turning to alcohol, drugs, or even suicide.

It is important to understand your angry feelings and why you have them. It is important to express them without hurting yourself or others. Depression is serious, and if you think you might be depressed, you need to seek professional help in order to overcome it. If depression is a problem for you, there are ways to get help.

Low self-esteem—a weak or negative sense of who you are as a person—is a root cause of depression.

Assessing Your Self-Esteem

Do you think your self-esteem is high or low? If you're not quite sure, take the following self-esteem test to find out. Be honest with your answers. Think about how you feel most of the time, not how you wish you felt, and answer either "true" or "false" to the statements below.

1. I like myself.
2. I believe in myself.
3. Others like me.
4. I like to meet new people.
5. I take criticism well.

6. I like to experience new things.
7. I can take the credit when I do something well.
8. Relationships are important to me.
9. I can share things with my family.
10. I am open about my feelings.
11. Seeing others do well makes me happy.
12. I think that I am a good person.
13. I am happy being me.

If you answered "true" to most of these statements, you have high self-esteem. If you answered "false" to most of them, your self-esteem could use some work. But don't feel bad about that. Recognizing that your self-esteem needs a boost is the first step toward improving it—and you've just done that!

Giving Your Self-Esteem a Lift

Improving your self-esteem will help you a lot when you are in a situation that is likely to make you angry. The first place to start is to take a good, honest look at yourself. List your good and bad points. Be proud of your good qualities, and work on those that are not so positive.

Accept Who You Are

You are who you are, whether you are tall or short, or average or beautiful. You can't change that, so stop complaining! Maybe you have nice skin, pretty eyes, or a terrific sense of humor. Concentrate on the things you like

Each of us has different strengths and weaknesses. Accepting our differences leads to improved self-esteem and a better, more positive outlook.

best about yourself, and think about all the qualities your family and friends like about you.

Don't Put Yourself Down

Stop telling yourself that you are stupid and can never do anything right. Instead, think about the things you are good at, and remember that even these things may have taken some time to achieve.

Learning to Accept Mistakes

If you have handled something poorly in the past, forgive yourself, but keep the mistake in mind and learn from it. Next time you will do better. Everyone makes mistakes— what matters is whether we learn from our mistakes or continue to make the same ones over and over again.

All in Good Time

Don't expect to wake up tomorrow morning with fantastic self-esteem. Making changes takes time. Go slowly and take the time you need to discover all the great things that make you a unique person.

Enjoy the Little Things

Do things that you enjoy. If lifting weights, going for a walk, or petting your cat makes you feel happy, then do it! Or, maybe just hang out with someone you care about and with whom you feel at ease. Being with happy and positive friends may make you feel better.

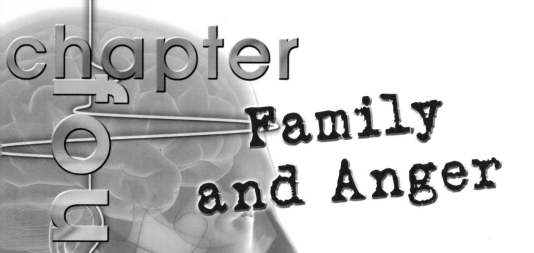

chapter four

Family and Anger

One of the most important influences in your life is your family. It may include your parents, stepparents, siblings, stepsiblings, cousins, and grandparents. The ideal family, no matter how the members are related to you, should create a safe, comfortable environment in which you are able to learn and grow.

Anger and Upbringing

How you react when you are angry depends on the type of

25

Strong emotional ties are the basis of family relationships. It is only natural that anger will come into play on occasion.

person you are. It also depends on how you were raised and how those around you deal with their own anger. But no matter what sort of behavior you are accustomed to, and no matter how angry you may feel, it is very important to control your anger and keep yourself from explosive outbursts.

While you were growing up, you may have received some confusing messages about your angry feelings. Parents don't always know how to react to a child's expressions of anger. If you did something like calling someone a cruel name or refusing to share your toys, your parents would probably say, "That's not a nice thing to do." But what about when you were angry? Did your parents get annoyed with you for expressing your feelings? Or, were you encouraged to speak your mind? Did you think any of these things when you were younger?

- It is wrong to feel anger.
- Only bad people get angry.
- If I show my anger, no one will like me.

Compare your answers by asking yourself how you feel about anger now that you're no longer a child.

- Do you keep your feelings to yourself?
- Do you feel guilty when you are mad at someone?
- Do you get upset when someone is angry with you?

Learning from Your Family

Your family has great influence on you. You learn many things from them. You are taught at home how to behave and how to treat other people. You learn the value of things like responsibility, honesty, and courage. You learn to make your own decisions and deal with your own problems. In many ways, the kind of person you will become depends largely upon your family. And, just as important, your family affects how you feel about yourself.

A healthy family fulfills certain needs of its members:

- The need to be loved
- The need for support and encouragement
- The need to express oneself
- The need to feel safe and secure

Even in the best of families, things are not always perfect. Family members do not always have to agree with each other. But they should care about each other. They should try to work things out through communication and compromise. The adults in a healthy family provide good role models for their children. A role model is someone who serves as an example—good or bad—for others.

Is there a lot of anger in your family? Do members of your family respond violently to anger? Are you in danger in your own home? If you answered "yes" to any of these questions, you need to get help. You may not be able to solve the problems at home, but you can get help for yourself.

There are many trained professionals who understand family problems. They know what you are going through, and they can help. At school, for example, you can talk to the nurse or counselor. You can also speak with a social worker or psychologist. Maybe you would feel comfortable talking with your family doctor or clergyperson. Talking can help. The more you understand about your family's problems, the better you will feel. There may be support groups in your area that deal with problems just like yours. Remember: don't let other people's anger bring you down! Even the family you love must not be allowed to hurt you.

Support groups give you an opportunity to talk to and hear from others who are dealing with issues similar to your own.

Ten Great Questions to Ask Your Therapist

1. Is there something wrong with me if I lose my temper all the time? Also, I frequently become angry at a level of intensity that is out of proportion to events. Is this normal?

2. How can I learn to deal with my emotions better?

3. How can I help a friend who can't manage his anger?

4. What should I do if I feel like I'm about to blow up?

5. I never feel angry about anything. Is there something wrong with me?

6. Sometimes, when I'm upset, I feel dizzy and short of breath. Is this normal?

7. What causes anger?

8. My parents lose their temper with me all the time. Is this normal?

9. How can I tell if I'm suffering from depression? What's the difference between depression and just feeling a little sad?

10. What's the best way to apologize to someone after a blowup?

chapter five

Understanding Your Anger

You have probably figured out by now that dealing with your anger, like many other things in life, is a balancing act. You've learned that it is not healthy to hold in your anger. You have also learned that it is not socially acceptable to express your anger in certain ways. It is harmful to use your anger to hurt other people or yourself. So, how are you supposed to deal with it?

Although it is not always easy, you can learn to control your anger and express it constructively. But as you can see from the increasing number of violent crimes that occur every day, uncontrolled anger can have disastrous results. Only you are responsible for the ways you express your anger.

Getting a Grip on Your Anger

Do you have a problem staying in control? Read the following questions. Answer them on a sheet of paper. See what your responses tell you about yourself.

1. Who makes you the most angry?
   - Parents
   - Siblings (brothers/ sisters/stepsiblings)
   - Teachers
   - Friends
   - Strangers

2. How do you usually respond when someone makes you angry?
   - Keep your feelings to yourself; don't let him or her know
   - Walk away; find someone to talk to
   - Tell him or her how you feel
   - Try to hurt him or her physically

In order to learn how to maintain control of your emotions, you need to recognize the people, things, and situations that typically make you upset.

- Take it out on someone else
- Plan to get even

3. How does your response make you feel?
   - Better, more calm
   - Wishing you had the nerve to say what you really feel
   - Confused, unable to think clearly
   - Ashamed of yourself, guilty
   - Nervous, afraid

4. What would you like to change about the way you express anger?
   - Nothing
   - Fight with words, instead of with your fists
   - Not let things bother you so much
   - Express your feelings more openly
   - Stay in control

Mood Swings

Do your moods change a lot? Mood fluctuation is normal for young adults, especially those whose hormones are changing due to puberty. It's even normal not to know why your moods change. If you are troubled by mood swings, try to look at the bright side of each situation that arises. This may take some practice.

Try the following exercise. On a piece of paper, finish the following sentences with positive thoughts. (Example: I have a broken arm, but I can still do lots of things with my other arm.)

1. I failed my midterm exam, but at finals I can . . .
2. My best friend is moving away, but I can still . . .
3. I forgot to bring money for lunch today, but I can still . . .
4. My parents work a lot, but I can still . . .
5. I didn't make the basketball team this year, but I can still . . .

Was that easy? Or, did you have a hard time coming up with something positive to complete each sentence? If you had a difficult time, try making up a few sentences of your own. Finding positive endings for bad situations is a good way to practice for when you are in a situation that might make you angry.

Let Go of Your Anger

Remind yourself that controlling your anger is possible. You may find these suggestions helpful.

Be Aware of Your Anger Reactions

Learn to recognize what happens to you as you become angry. There are a few warning signs of anger, and when you see that they are present, they should serve as a reminder to you to do anger-reducing activities such as deep breathing. Ask yourself: Am I grinding my teeth, or feeling tightness in my stomach? Is my heart beating faster? Am I avoiding eye contact?

Maybe you do things when you are angry that you don't normally do. Overeating, smoking, and drinking

Meditation and deep-breathing exercises are proven ways to work through feelings of anger. Dwelling on positive things for even a few minutes a day can be useful.

are some of the things some people do when they are mad. Maybe you become sarcastic and make fun of those around you. Whatever happens, pay attention to your reaction. Tell yourself that it is happening because you are feeling angry. You may lose control if you don't pay attention to your anger. Angry feelings don't go away by themselves. They can build up inside you and get even stronger. If you tend to keep angry feelings to yourself, it is likely that someday the bottled-up anger could explode without warning.

Getting to the Source

You know yourself pretty well. Think about the things that bother you. Make a list of issues that you are sensitive about. Include in your list people who can "push your buttons." Who really gets to you? Are you upset by an alcoholic parent, a disability, or an illness in the family? Who or what makes you feel threatened?

Know your limits. How much can you take? How long can you hold yourself back? It is important to find out before you do something that you will be sorry about later.

MYTHS AND FACTS

Myth: Anger is always wrong and unjustifiable.

Fact: There are times when anger is definitely justified. For example, if you have been betrayed by a boyfriend or girlfriend, or if you have been physically attacked by someone, anger is a natural response. After all, there is a biological explanation for your anger. Anger gets your adrenaline going—it activates the fight-or-flight response, an in-born response to threat—that kept early humans on their toes. Biologically speaking, anger spurs you into action.

Myth: Angry people are easy to pick out of a crowd.

Fact: Most people with anger management problems appear quite calm until they explode.

Myth: Anger is inevitable—it can't be helped.

Fact: Although anger is an instinctual response that our early ancestors no doubt called upon for survival, it is a state that can be controlled. Anger is a complex emotion that is often triggered by feelings of fear, frustration, helplessness, and confusion. Positive solutions to solving problems can help a person control his or her anger.

chapter six

Managing Your Anger

How you choose to examine the various elements that make up your world is called your attitude. There's an old saying that a positive outlook leads to a positive outcome. If you have a positive attitude and look on the bright side of things, you may find that you are in control of your anger and react well to bad situations. But if you generally have a negative attitude and focus on the problems or difficulties in any given situation, you may find problems wherever you go and get angry rather quickly.

Regaining Control

Lashing out may feel good for a brief moment, but using violence is never a good way to resolve your anger. Violence will only cause more problems. You should find more positive and healthy ways to control your anger. Here are a few suggestions.

Give yourself a few moments to cool off before responding to someone who has just angered you.

- Take a deep breath and relax.
- Walk away from the situation and come back when you are feeling more in control.
- Count to ten before you say something that you might regret.
- Stop and think of three ways to handle the situation before you react.
- Talk it out.

These techniques are most effective when used early on in a situation that has the potential to become heated. Being aware of early warning signs can be a useful reminder to use these techniques. By using these strategies and others like them, you, too, can control your anger.

Using Your Anger Constructively

Have you ever been angry because you did not like the way that you or somebody else was being treated? Has anything ever seemed so unfair that you got angry and decided to do something about it? When you use your anger constructively, it can inspire you to improve your life and make a change in the world.

Turn things around and make them work for you. For example, if somebody is rude to you, use your anger constructively to let that person know how you feel. In fact, most people with anger problems are terrible at expressing their feelings or being assertive. Consequently, these feelings build up over time, eventually leading to explosive outbursts like those of a pressure cooker. If littering and pollution frustrate you, use your anger to start a campaign to clean up your neighborhood or city.

Learning how to recognize, interpret, and, ultimately, express your

When people direct their anger at you, one wrong move can escalate the situation. Try to be the "cooler head" that prevails.

feelings in a positive and constructive way takes time. There are ways for you to harness the anger you feel. For instance, you know instinctively that if someone confronts you at a traffic signal and accuses you of cutting him or her off, you should try to defuse the situation, no matter how angry you yourself may be. After all, the other person in this situation may be dangerous. You can quell your anger and the other driver's by maintaining your manners. Apologize and ask him or her what you can do to help. What's more important here? Releasing the anger you're feeling, or preventing a potentially dangerous situation?

Getting Help

If your anger is too much for you to handle on your own, help is available. The good news is that there are many research-proven anger management techniques that are easy to learn and effective with practice. Conflict resolution is a popular method of problem solving used in schools. It teaches students how to work out angry feelings. The goal of conflict resolution is to end conflicts before they start or lead to physical confrontation or fighting. A mediator at a conflict resolution meeting will objectively consider each side's needs. Then, he or she will try to find a solution that satisfies each person at least a little. It is an excellent way to diffuse anger and teach people how to deal with angry people they may encounter in their daily lives.

You may also want to talk to your parents or family members, neighbors, friends, a teacher, a school social worker or counselor, a doctor, or a religious adviser. You may also look in the Yellow Pages of your local phone book to find:

- Counseling services for individuals and families
- Mental health centers or social service centers
- YMCA/YWCA
- Psychologists

It is up to you to take the first step. And though it may be difficult, go right ahead—it's the best thing you can do for yourself!

When it comes to controlling your anger, words are important. Try to talk openly about your feelings with the person who has made you angry.

Telling Somebody How You Feel

It may be a good idea for you to tell the person responsible for your anger how you feel. You should do this in an assertive way by not placing blame on somebody else but by taking responsibility for your reactions to others. For example, you can say things such as, "It made me mad when you . . ." or "I am angry because . . ." This can start people talking. Sometimes, it clears the air. You might come to an understanding, and the anger that you feel may disappear.

Taking Control

Don't give up on yourself. You will "blow it" once in a while. Everyone does. The important thing is to understand why you lost control. Ask yourself what you did wrong and how you can do better next time.

You must decide that you want to be in control of your anger. Take responsibility for how you express your feelings. And start practicing the things that will help calm you down. Maybe it's a few words to yourself: "This is not a big deal." Whatever it is, try to remember to use it as much as possible. Then start working toward your goal.

abuse Use of violence or emotional pain to control another person.

compromise Way to settle differences by having both parties make concessions; give-and-take.

demeanor Outward bearing or behavior.

depression Mental illness with a combination of symptoms that interfere with a person's ability to function normally and experience pleasure.

escalate To increase or rise.

fight-or-flight response Instinct brought about by a threatening situation that motivates people either to run away or fight in order to protect themselves.

grudge Long-standing feeling of anger and resentment.

hostile Openly opposed and combative.

irritable Easily excited or annoyed.

juvenile Young person.

notorious Widely and unfavorably known; infamous.

paranoid Extremely fearful or suspicious.

passive-aggressive behavior When a person expresses his or her anger in subtle and indirect ways.

prejudice Baseless attitude of anger or hostility directed toward an individual.

psychologist Person who studies the mind and behavior.

recklessly Without proper care or attention.

self-esteem How a person feels about him- or herself.

silent treatment Not talking or communicating with somebody on purpose to express anger.

stress Physical and mental strain that occurs when we react to any kind of demand.

support group Gathering in which people who face the same problems meet and talk about their issues.

American Psychological Association (APA)
750 First Street NE
Washington, DC 20002-4242
(800) 374-2721
Web site: http://www.apa.org/pubinfo/anger.html
The APA seeks to better the science and practice of psychology.
With a membership of 150,000, it is the largest association of
psychologists in the world.

Center for the Prevention of School Violence
1801 Mail Service Center
Raleigh, NC 27699-1801
(800) 299-6054
Web site: http://www.ncdjjdp.org/cpsv
This national organization runs a resource center and does advocacy
work to address bullying and violence in schools.

National Institute of Mental Health (NIMH)
Public Information and Communications Branch
6001 Executive Boulevard, Room 8184, MSC 9663
Bethesda, MD 20892-9663
(866) 615-6464
Web site: http://www.nimh.nih.gov
A part of the National Institutes of Health, the NIMH is an
organization that leads government research of mental health and
behavioral disorders. The institute also develops and operates a
variety of outreach programs.

National Youth Violence Prevention
        Resource Center (NYVPRC)
P.O. Box 10809

Rockville, MD 20849-0809
(866) SAFEYOU (723-3968)
Web site: http://www.safeyouth.org
Established by the Centers for Disease Control and Prevention and other federal agencies, the center acts as a gateway for young people, parents, professionals, and other concerned individuals to programs, tools, and information regarding youth violence.

TeenHelp.org
Web site: http://www.teenhelp.org
TeenHelp.org is a Web site dedicated to giving sound advice to teens on just about everything. With more than twenty-five thousand teen members, it offers a support forum as well as counsel from more than one hundred e-mail mentors.

Teen Line
Cedars-Sinai Medical Center
P.O. Box 48750
Los Angeles, CA 90048
(310) 855-4673 (HOPE)
Web site: http://www.teenlineonline.org
Established in 1981, Teen Line offers teen-to-teen support on the issues they face. From 6:00 PM to 10:00 PM (PST), teens who need to talk are encouraged to call the hotline.

TeensHealth.org
Web site: http://www.teenshealth.org/teen
This organization offers advice on a variety of emotional issues tailored for teens.

YMCA of the USA
101 North Wacker Drive

Chicago, IL 60606
(312) 977-0031
Web site: http://www.ymca.net
With more than 2,500 locations nationwide, the YMCA readily offers
teens accessible counseling and coping resources.

Web Sites

Due to the changing nature of Internet links, Rosen
Publishing has developed an online list of Web sites
related to the subject of this book. This site is updated
regularly. Please use this link to access the list:

http://www.rosenlinks.com/tmh/aaam

for further reading

Carlson, Richard. *Don't Sweat the Small Stuff for Teens.*
New York, NY: Hyperion, 2000.

Hershorn, Michael. *Cool It! Teen Tips to Keep Hot Tempers from Boiling Over.* Far Hills, NJ: New Horizon Press: 2003.

McKay, Gary D., and Steven A. Maybell. *Calming the Family Storm: Anger Management for Moms, Dads, and All the Kids.* Atascadero, CA: Impact Publishers, 2004.

McKay, Matthew, Peter Rogers, and Judith McKay. *When Anger Hurts.* 2nd ed. New York, NY: New Harbinger Publications, 2003.

Roberts, Anita. *SafeTeen: Powerful Alternatives to Violence.* Toronto, Canada: Polestar Book Publishers, 2001.

Seaward, Brian, and Linda Bartlett. *Hot Stones and Funny Bones: Teens Helping Teens Cope with Stress and Anger.* Deerfield Beach, FL: HCI Teens, 2002.

About the Author

Charlie Quill is an author and journalist living in Buffalo, New York. In the course of conducting research for *Anger and Anger Management*, he consulted with several noted mental health professionals who study anger and witness on a daily basis the destructive consequences of this powerful human emotion.

Photo Credits

Cover, p. 1 (top left) © www.istockphoto.com/Jason Stitt; cover, p. 1 (middle left, bottom left) © www.istockphoto.com; cover, pp. 1, 3 (foreground) © www.istockphoto.com/Jason Stitt; cover, pp. 1, 3 (head) © www.istockphoto.com; pp. 4, 12, 25, 30, 36 (books) © www.istockphoto.com/Michal Koziarski; p. 4 © www.istockphoto.com/Nicholas Manu; pp. 5, 26, 34, 38 © Getty Images; p. 7 © www.istockphoto.com/Csaba Fikker; p. 8 © Sean O'Brien/Custom Medical Stock Photo; p. 10 © www.istockphoto.com; p. 12 © www.istockphoto.com/Jason Lugo; p. 14 © Universal/Courtesy Everett Collection; p. 16 © Courtesy NBC/ZUMA Press; p. 19 © www.istockphoto.com/Quavondo Nguyen; p. 21 © www.istockphoto.com/Robert Dodge; p. 23 © www.istockphoto.com/Andrea Gingerich; p. 25 © www.istockphoto.com/Tracy Whiteside; p. 28 © Kevin Beebe/Custom Medical Stock Photo; p. 30 © www.istockphoto.com; p. 31 © www.istockphoto.com/Heather Wall; p. 36 © www.istockphoto.com/Bonnie Schupp; p. 37 © www.istockphoto.com/Izabela Habur; p. 40 © Bob Pardue/Alamy.

Designer: Nelson Sá; Editor: Christopher Roberts
Photo Researcher: Marty Levick